Christmas in the Philippines

by Cheryl L. Enderlein

Content Consultants:
Maria Elizabeth F. Garcia, Assistant Cultural Officer
Eduardo Maglaya, Consul General
Embassy of the Philippines

Hilltop Books

An Imprint of Franklin Watts
A Division of Grolier Publishing
New York   London   Hong Kong   Sydney
Danbury, Connecticut

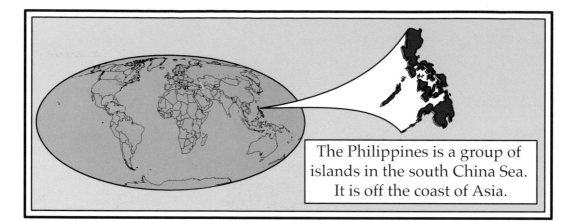

The Philippines is a group of islands in the south China Sea. It is off the coast of Asia.

Hilltop Books
http://publishing.grolier.com
Copyright © 1998 by Capstone Press • All rights reserved
Published simultaneously in Canada• Printed in the United States of America

Library of Congress Cataloging-in-Publication Data
Enderlein, Cheryl L.
    Christmas in the Philippines/by Cheryl L. Enderlein.
    p. cm.--(Christmas around the world)
    Includes bibliographical references and index.
    Summary: Briefly describes the customs, songs, foods, and activities associated with the celebration of Christmas in the Philippines.
    ISBN 1-56065-623-9
    1. Christmas--Philippines--Juvenile literature. 2. Christmas decorations--Philippines--Juvenile literature. 3. Philippines--Social life and customs--Juvenile literature. [1. Christmas--Philippines. 2. Philippines--Social life and customs.] I. Title. II. Series.
GT4987.76.E53   1998
394.2663'09599--dc21

                              97-11341
                                 CIP
                                 AC

Photo credits
Veronica Garbutt, 10
Ernest Jones, 16
Patrick Lucero, 6, 18
Philippine Convention and Visitors Corporation, 4
George Tapan, cover, 8, 12, 14, 20

Table of Contents

Christmas in the Philippines 5

The First Christmas 7

Symbols of Christmas 9

Decorations 11

Christmas Celebrations 13

Holiday Foods 15

Lolo and Lola 17

Christmas Presents 19

Christmas Songs 21

Hands On: Make a Parol 22

Words to Know 23

Read More 24

Useful Addresses and Internet Sites 24

Index 24

Christmas in the Philippines

Christmas is a holiday that is celebrated around the world. Celebrate means to do something enjoyable on a special occasion. People in different countries celebrate Christmas in different ways.

The Philippines is a group of more than 7,100 islands. The islands are off the coast of Asia. They are in the south China Sea. People from the Philippines are called Filipinos. They speak Filipino. Their Christmas greeting is Maligayang Pasko (mah-lee-GAH-yang pahs-KOH). It means Merry Christmas.

Christmas Day is always celebrated on December 25. But celebrations in the Philippines start on December 16. The celebrating lasts until around the first Sunday of January.

Christmas time in the Philippines is usually the coolest time of the year. It is usually about 70 degrees Fahrenheit (about 21 degress Celcius).

Filipinos buy Christmas decorations for their homes.

The First Christmas

Many Christmas celebrations are part of the Christian religion. A religion is a set of beliefs people follow. Christians are people who follow the teachings of Jesus Christ. They celebrate Christmas as Jesus' birthday.

Jesus' mother was Mary. She was married to Joseph. Mary and Joseph traveled to the city of Bethlehem. They could not find any room at the inns. An inn is like a hotel. Mary and Joseph had to stay in a stable. A stable is where animals are kept.

Jesus was born in the stable. His first bed was a manger. A manger is a food box for animals. The manger was filled with straw.

Wise men brought gifts for Jesus. They followed a bright star. The star led them to Jesus.

Many Christmas celebrations remind people of the first Christmas. Many celebrations in the Philippines are Christian.

Filipinos set up figures to remember the Christmas story.

Symbols of Christmas

The star lantern is a Christmas symbol in the Philippines. A symbol is something that stands for another thing. Filipinos call the star lantern a parol (pah-ROLL). A parol is a five-pointed star inside of a circle. It is made out of bamboo and bright paper. Bamboo is a plant with a hollow stem. There is usually a candle or light inside the parol.

Filipinos start making parols two or three months before Christmas. The men and boys cut the bamboo. People bend the bamboo into frames of different sizes. The women and girls cut paper. They glue the paper to the bamboo frame. Each point of the star has a tassel. A tassel is a bunch of yarn or ribbon. It is tied together at the top.

Parols hang everywhere in the Philippines during the Christmas season. They are found in houses, stores, and churches. They remind many Filipinos of the star the wise men followed.

Men and women work together to make parols.

Decorations

People in the Philippines decorate their houses for Christmas. Most Filipinos put up Christmas trees.

There are very few evergreen trees in the Philippines. An evergreen tree is a tree that is always green. Instead, many Filipinos have fake evergreen trees. Some have a palm tree branch in a pot. Others make trees from cardboard or twigs. A twig is a small branch.

Filipinos place ornaments on their trees. An ornament is a decoration. Some Filipinos use candy and fruit. Shells and bamboo shapes are other common ornaments.

Parols are one of the most popular Christmas decorations. Families hang them in all their windows. They also decorate the outside of their homes with parols.

Most Filipinos put up fake Christmas trees.

Christmas Celebrations

Filipinos have many fiestas (fee-ES-tahs) during the year. A fiesta is a special celebration or holiday. One favorite fiesta is Christmas.

The Christmas season starts on December 16. Church bells wake people up at four o'clock in the morning. Filipinos get up and go to church. The service is called Misa de Gallo (MEE-suh deh GAHL-yoh). The words mean Mass of the Rooster. A mass is a church service. It is called the Mass of the Rooster because it is held so early. Roosters crow early in the morning.

Every morning for nine days people go to church. They go to church to pray. On Christmas Eve, people go to Midnight Mass. Then they go home for a family feast. The feast is called Noche Buena (NOH-chay BWAY-nuh).

Most Filipinos celebrate Christmas by attending special masses.

Holiday Foods

Filipinos serve Noche Buena buffet style. Buffet means all the food is set on a table. People go to the table to fill their plates. There are about 15 kinds of food.

Filipinos eat chicken and rice soup at the feast. They also have spring rolls stuffed with meat and vegetables. A spring roll is like an egg roll. Filipinos eat fish and chicken stuffed with ham and pork. They have noodle dishes and many kinds of fruit. There are many kinds of dessert, too.

The favorite Christmas dessert in the Philippines is bibingka (bee-BING-kah). A bibingka is a Philippine pancake made from rice flour. It is cooked with milk, cheese, and duck eggs. It is served in a banana leaf. The leaf is like a plate. Filipinos top the bibingka with coconut and brown sugar. They drink ginger tea with dessert.

There are about 15 kinds of food at the Noche Buena feast.

Lolo and Lola

Lolo (LOH-loh) and Lola (LOH-lah) are important people in the Christmas celebration. Lolo means grandfather. Lola means grandmother. They are like Santa Claus in North America.

Children in the Philippines know about Santa Claus. They see pictures of Santa. But Santa is not a big part of the Filipino Christmas. He does not bring gifts.

During the family feast, Lolo and Lola give gifts to their grandchildren. They usually make giving the gifts into a game. For one game, they gather all the grandchildren together in a circle. Then they throw gold coins in the air. The children rush to get the money.

Lola gives gifts to her grandchildren during the family feast.

Christmas Presents

People all over the world give gifts at Christmas. Giving gifts reminds Christians of the wise men's gifts. The wise men brought special gifts to Jesus when he was born.

Children in the Philippines receive gifts from Lolo and Lola. People in families also give gifts to one another. The gifts are simple and practical. Practical means something useful. Clothes are a practical gift. Many Filipino children receive new clothes for Christmas. They wear new clothes to Midnight Mass.

After church, Noche Buena begins. The party lasts all night. No one goes to bed. Children start visiting their family members when it is daylight. They usually receive a gift at each house. It might be a toy or money or candy.

An all-night party begins after church on Christmas Eve.

Christmas Songs

Singing Christmas songs is a popular holiday activity. Both young and old people take part in the singing. They sing every night starting on December 16. They sing some Filipino songs and some English ones. They walk through the streets singing songs.

Some towns have groups of singers called pastores (pahs-TOHR-ees). Pastore means shepherd. The people in the group sing and dance. They wear costumes. They sing Christmas songs.

In the cities, groups of children called cumbancheros (kum-ban-CHAY-rohs) walk around their neighborhoods. They go from house to house singing Christmas songs. Cumbancheros play musical instruments. Often the instruments are homemade. People give them coins. The children share the coins they collect.

Cumbancheros sing and play musical instruments.

Hands On: Make a Parol

Make a parol like the ones Filipinos make. You can make it without the lantern in the middle.

What You Need
Five popsicle sticks
Small paper plate
Ribbon or yarn

Glue stick
Markers, crayons, or glitter

What You Do
1. Make a five-pointed star using the popsicle sticks. To make a star, pick two sticks. Glue one end of one stick to one end of the other stick. The unglued ends should be two inches (five centimeters) apart. Do the same thing with two other sticks.
2. Number the ends of each stick in each V. Number them 1, 2, 3, 4. Glue the end you have numbered 1 to the end you have numbered 4. There should be two inches (five centimeters) between the ends of the Vs.
3. Glue the ends of your last stick to the ends numbered 2 and 3. Glue it under the rest of your star.
4. When your star is dry, decorate it with markers or crayons. You can use glitter, too.
5. Glue the star to a small paper plate. If you want, you can also decorate the plate.
6. Put the ribbon or yarn on each of the star's points. You can make bows or streamers.
7. Hang your parol in a window or on your Christmas tree.

Words to Know

Christian (KRISS-chuhn)—a person who follows the teachings of Jesus Christ

evergreen (EV-ur-green)—a tree that stays green all the time

inn (IN)—a place to sleep overnight like a hotel

manger (MAYN-jur)—a food box for animals

mass (MASS)—a church service

ornament (OR-nuh-muhnt)—a decoration hung on a Christmas tree

parol (pah-ROLL)—a star-shaped lantern made out of bamboo and colored paper

stable (STAY-buhl)—a building for animals like a barn

Read More

Cuyler, Margery. *The All-Around Christmas Book*. New York: Holt, Rinehart and Winston, 1982.

Fowler, Virginie. *Christmas Crafts and Customs*. Englewood Cliffs, N.J.: Prentice-Hall, 1984.

Lankford, Mary D. *Christmas Around the World*. New York: Morrow Junior Books, 1995.

World Book. *Christmas in the Philippines*. Chicago: World Book, Inc., 1990.

Useful Addresses and Internet Sites

The Embassy of the Philippines
1600 Massachusetts Avenue NW
Washington, DC 20036

Philippine Association
425 Madison Avenue
New York, NY 10017

Christmas.com
http://www.christmas.com
Christmas 'round the World
http://www.auburn.edu/%7Evestmon/christmas.html
A Worldwide Christmas Calendar
http://www.algonet.se/~bernadot/christmas/info.html

Index

bamboo, 9, 11
bibingka, 15
Christmas tree, 11
cumbancheros, 21
evergreens, 11
Jesus, 7, 19
Lola, 17, 19
Lolo, 17, 19
Maligayang Pasko, 5

manger, 7
Midnight Mass, 13
Misa de Gallo, 13
Noche Buena, 13, 15, 19
ornament, 11
parol, 9, 11
pastores, 21
stable, 7
wise men, 7, 9, 19